You Among the Flowers

Kahōkūlani

BookLeaf Publishing

Presentation by *BookLeaf Publishing*

Web: www.bookleafpub.com

E-mail: info@bookleafpub.com

ISBN: 9789357440639

First edition 2023

DEDICATION

To my sunflower. Thank you for lighting my world even on the darkest of days.

And to all of you who have experienced love's joys and heartache. It's valid to feel all that you do. Keep your heart open and love yourself unconditionally.

ACKNOWLEDGEMENT

Thank you to my family and friends that have supported my craft throughout my life and have pushed me beyond my limits to find the words to capture the human experience.

At the end of the day, we are but words, so thank you for allowing me the space to string a few together for you all.

Cover design by Tiara Rivera

PREFACE

My creativity was in a deep slumber for years and one person 2800 miles away inspired me to write again. I was challenged to find my voice and write a poem. "Sunflower" was a result of that undertaking and it marked the beginning of my heart's unexpected journey of love and healing.

These 20 poems and 1 open letter express the emotional highs and lows I've experienced - a love that came out of nowhere. A love that mirrors my soul and set me on a course for self-reflection.

I hope that a line or two resonate with you and my words inspire you to continue to evolve as a person who is ready to receive light and love.

it's you

you breathe life into me,
so let me make you live forever.
let me give you an eternity on ink-stamped paper
so everyone after me will know your love gave
me language.

sunflower

resting between the inflections of your voice,
following them up and down discerning what
you mean.
imagining a smile, maybe a raised eyebrow
accompanied by a soft look.
the voice of a daydream.

i long to wander the sunflower fields of your
mind, uncovering the deepest parts of you,
the you that rarely comes to light.
if i'm to come along for the journey, i'd like to
understand where you've been,
what motivates you, what is it that you delight?

who are you truly? dog lover. nurturer. taurus.
many skim the surface and fall for the projected
you not knowing what it is you desire.
what keeps you up at night that you pour your
hot tea so sleepily in the morning?
what in life and love do you require?

you hint with subtle glimpses through choice
words and photos thrusting my curiosity
forward.

the excitement with each received message
tickles my senses further.
how much more am i uncovering?
what is it that we are moving toward?

a natural end causes a pause and i find myself
hurdling the time constraint
trying to outrun the inevitable shift from day to
night,
before you go, undress your soul for me, sing me
a song nobody else has heard,
and give me a lasting glance as if there is
nobody else in sight.

as you rest, i sit and ponder how your eyes hold
stories i have yet to learn.
what's beyond the flirtatious batting that draws
your audience closer?
are you chasing passion? fleeing sadness?
rebuilding and healing from the time that you
chose her?

are you looking outward hoping to be seen?
unravel with me, tell me everything, beginning,
end, and all in between.

oracle

there's something so familiar about you.
there's a sense of belonging.
stalling, not knowing what to do,
and i will just be prolonging

the need for conversation,
exchanging our thoughts.
looking to you for confirmation,
i overthink, trying to connect the dots.

the oracle reads you're a kindred spirit,
but it feels like so much more.
deeper than any definition can fit it,
something celestial? fantasy? of lore?

it's almost beyond comprehension,
yet it's right in front of us.
i need to give this my attention.
i know that i must.

but how do i maintain an innocent feeling?
i feel too entangled at the moment.
as if my smile wasn't already revealing.
considering the need for atonement.

so i'll bite my cheeks and clench my jaw
to stop me from telling you how deeply i feel.
it's passionate, it's immense, and raw,
but once i say it, it will be real.

birthday poem

wherever this goes, whatever we will be,
i will be by your side wholeheartedly.

there will never be a time when you doubt my words,
never a time where you question my actions.
i will evolve and transform into whatever you want,
and perhaps then,

a time will come when it can be me,
a time when you will be free,
to let your wild spirit roam
and i can be the anchor that you call home.

bathtub - june depression

let the sage cloud my space.
clear all this anxiety, jealousy,
it's peace that i crave.

i submerge my body hoping to drown out the
feelings of the outside world.
i can't handle their emotions on top of mine.

i feel congested.

she's touched you, but i feel dirty.
i'm cold in hot water, feeling unworthy.
bathing in tears and soap, i'm weightless and
heavy.
don't let me swallow the murkiness,
silence could be deadly.

you're an empath, but you couldn't feel me?
"we're just friends right?" *sends smile emoji.
"i'm happy if you are," trying so hard to hide it
well,
but i must have, you didn't sense my personal
hell.

having to keep it quiet, trying to forget.
feeling stuck on the sidelines, wishing we hadn't
met.

because why is it even alright for me to feel this
way?
and you continue to send pictures as if
everything is okay.
as if you didn't just press your lips on somebody
else.
as if you didn't just place me back on the shelf.
as if this didn't diminish my mental health.
as if all of this couldn't have been helped.
but i know, that i did this,
to myself.

run away #1 (overwhelmed)

on the outside looking in -
why am i not on the table?
what do they have that i don't?
what can they do, that i'm unable?

am i not worthy of your heart?
i've only ever opened mine.
why am i even thinking this way?
this couldn't happen at a worst time.

saturated in my own tears on the way home.
i can't even cry in peace.
what do i even say? that it's work stress?
lies! i can't deny this grief.

your tears follow mine,
trailing down and burning skin.
i don't want you to cry for me.
it's not your fault i feel agony within.

so what now?
space hurts. i don't know what to do or say.
i can't imagine losing our daily streak,
but i'm in pain, suffering, every day.

i just want it to be you
more than anything because you see me.
you've been in the cold, in the dark, and alone.
you understand my need to be free

from all that's holding me back
unlike anyone else.
that's why it's so hard to let go,
but i just want you for myself.

in reality, i'm not even available.
i live too far away, already settled.
but god, i would uproot my life for this.
confusion in my mind, i'm heavily disheveled.

i feel all too much and nothing.
i recluse, "just leave me alone."
i try to convince myself to let you be.
but i'm weak. so i pick up the phone.

open letter

i hope when this reaches you, your heart, body, mind, and soul are in harmony. i hope the pain of your past doesn't consume you and that i can fill you with joy and put you at ease, even if it's just the second you start reading. i want to remind you that i will fight alongside you every moment you find yourself stressed, hurt, whether it's physically or emotionally, when the anxiety creeps in and depression tries to make a home within you. i know what it's like to be in combat with yourself every day. i know that you need to heal all the fragmented pieces of you and i won't let the rest shatter. i want us to continue finding comfort in one another and give each other hope that one day we won't carry this emotional distress on our backs. one day the yellow of a sunflower will be much brighter, we'll sing with the birds, and find the rain to be beautiful as it washes away our sorrow. there's nobody in this universe who understands me the way you do. and i see you too. i see the young girl looking to be protected and loved. she needs a love that is consistent and unconditional. a love that won't abandon or neglect her. i can sense that she never enjoyed the little things because her world became too complicated, confusing, and cold. a world where lollipops didn't taste the same and rainbows grew dark. i truly see pieces of myself in you. i know we have the strength to get through each day. i know little you and little me will find the serenity we've been looking for and never fear that the monsters will come while we sleep. we're underneath all that violence and chaos. we'll pull each other out of these pits and finally find the peace and happiness we deserve. it may hurt and be scary as hell to face everything in the shadows, so don't let go of my hand. we will find a way and come out on the other side loving ourselves through and through. and just know, that i will always be by your side and i will always look after you. forever and ever.

run away #2 (grieving)

i'm grieving something that doesn't exist.
i can't keep smiling as this bruising persists.

how can you be okay with "whatever this is?"
don't you feel as i do? what did i miss?

i can't talk to you anymore. i feel like only you have gained.
i'm collapsing and i'm fucking emotionally drained.

i hope whoever holds your heart knows where to begin.
what to say and how to love you, all with pure intention.

forever is not an easy promise. don't feel bad for moving forward.
i need to walk away for me. i need to sever the cord.

i don't know how long i need to find my light once more.

i've burned all that i had for you. i've depleted
my core.

i thought i could hold on and be all that you
need.
but now i'm empty, i'm numb, there's nothing left
to bleed.

i know you're not stringing me along, but that's
how i feel.
i just want to turn all this off. i don't want this to
be real.

i can't fathom life without you, but i can't be one
of three.
so goodbye for now, i'm doing this for me.

synchronicities (you're everywhere)

sunflowers follow me wherever i go,
on the bins of the plane, the most random place.
hanging from a rearview mirror at costco,
its sunny disposition dangling in my face.

a lion mural surrounded by sunflowers,
a politician's sign drenched in morning dew,
painted on the side of a rooster, it finds me at all hours,
pushing me to find my way back to you.

i drop my phone and "yellow" begins to play.
i'm rerouted to a street with a garden.
all the sunflowers stand tall midday,
reminding me to finish what i started.

my cards say i've been impatient, i'm
abandoning you, and i'm being unfair,
that we have a soul connection, not to give up,
no one else can compare.

bumble bees

i look at them wishing it was you,
vibes are great at dinner, but something feels off.
my mind and heart don't know what to do,
i feel your presence subtle and soft.

sometimes i hear songs that bring my thoughts
back.
i find myself thinking of your voice.
i can't help but pause and listen to the track,
my body gives me no choice.

there always seems to be a roadblock
when i start talking to them.
sometimes the timing is off
and the conversations just end.

it's as if the universe doesn't want me to forget
and doesn't want me to leave.
i'm loyal without having to commit.
my heart unwilling to receive

love from anybody else
because it doesn't feel the same.
but maybe i'm just holding back myself
although my heart's been claimed.

i don't think i had any control.
this is just one of life's dealings.
this is an eternal contract of the soul
and there's no stopping these feelings.

run away #3 (impatient)

i'm triggered.
projecting childhood family dynamics onto you.
and my karmic relations have nothing to do with us.
yet here i am, feeling abandoned, not enough, vulnerable, unprotected.

you can't keep us here forever,
rip the bandaid, choose. so i can feel better.

i'm attacking you and spitting fire,
fighting with all that i have because you're the one i desire.

i can't wait anymore, please just fucking say it!
tell me it's not me, i know that i can take it.

i rather be rejected than dwell in the unknown.
i'm gasping for air in panic, just fucking let me go.

the anxiety is brewing, my blood boils, and i'm heavy.
just spit it out, this impatience is hard to carry.

i'm so up and down. i know this ride is wavy.
i'm drowning in hopes and dreams, say
something to save me.

it's been 8 months, how do you not know?
what the hell are we doing? where do we go?

everyone around me seems to be lost on their
choice.
am i carrying that energy here? have i lost my
own voice?

i can't discern if this is really me.
but it feels real, the sadness, impatience, i'm
angry.

i just want to shake it out of you. what are you
not saying?
what do you gain from all of this delaying?

it's obvious, is it not? anyone would pick me.
why is this difficult? should i cycle back and
grieve?

i don't understand why you can't decide.
do you really love me? what is it that you're
trying to hide?

you say you don't want to hurt anyone, but
really you don't want to hurt yourself.
what if you lose us all and we find somebody
else?

but maybe you rather us leave than for you to
have a say.
it's selfish to not speak up just to avoid that day.

at some point someone's heart will break.
yours? mine? or whoever else is at stake.

i'm pleading and you don't know what to do.
emojis for responses. really? fuck this, i wanna
un-know you.

from my ego

choose me because i make you feel alive.
because with me, it's okay to feel, to be angry, to cry.

the people closest to you hurt you, but you're safe with me.
i see your scars. i've walked with those demons.
you know i won't leave.

choose me because i ignite your passion for life, for art, to pursue all that you desire.
i give you space to be, to create, there's no shame in what you aspire.

choose me because i push you outside your bubble to try new things and grow.
you thrive with me, you're happier, more open, and it shows.

there is nothing i won't do to help you succeed.
i will be there for every challenge, every smile, tear, whatever you need.

choose me because you know what is in my heart and soul.

you can feel me from there, you know i make
you whole.

i will always listen, validate, and be true to my
words.
choose me because i'm the only one your heart
deserves.

infinite

immediate recognition without knowing how.
endlessly falling between each syllable spoken.
my soul dancing in every conversation,
finding beauty in the broken.

forever in awe that someone pure exists.
mirroring all my shadows and being my light.
giving me warmth and comfort, you help me
find my strength,
i'm grounded and balanced when nothing feels
right.

time and distance are illusions.
i carry you with me miles away.
i feel your energy vibrate within me,
but the longing grows for that "one day."

my skin will touch yours soon enough,
sensations of lightning throughout.
the divine union finally manifested.
a coming of home no doubt.

we've lived as halves in separation,
journeyed without the other.

life is shifting around us, bringing us into this
space
to be whatever need to be for one another.

our capacity to love, to heal, and to understand is
infinite.
we give each other emotional safety and
security.
we love without conditions, no judgements.
authentically just you and me.

body

your soft casing radiates the lover within.
i see the warmth of your spirit in your cheeks.
your inner thoughts dance on your tender lips.
sadness has touched your eyes and yet they still see light in every corner.
your hair has changed as you have – each curl has grown with you in all of your phases.
your breasts, full and delicate, remind you of your body's cycles. she too goes through changes.
your hips glide side to side as you wander. listen to them when they say you are not lost. they are taking you where you're meant to be.
your hands create a world of your choosing, bringing the beauty of your art into the physical realm.
pause your breath every once in a while and allow it to soothe any disharmony inside as it settles into your lungs.
your heart, a resilient device, although tattered and used, still beats life into you waiting for you to open up again.
each part of you, in rhythmic motion, works together to adorn the world with your existence.
while every curve i have yet to touch outlines the beautiful soul i fell in love with.

self check-in

how am i feeling right now?
are my affirmations working?
is my shadow work done?
are those demons still lurking?

have i forgiven my past?
is my inner child at peace?
have i shed my ego?
is there more to release?

have i reached my highest self?
the best version of me?
do i feel complete on my own?
am i living authentically?

do i feel fulfilled in all areas of life?
can i be happy without her?
can i be everything i need for myself?
can i count on my strength to not falter?

can i cope when i'm triggered?
do i have enough skills?
and if i find sadness again,
can i handle how that feels?

am i balanced, grounded, and aligned?
can i be consistent with self-care?
will i keep creating?
can i stay self-aware?

have i learned all of my lessons?
am i confident enough to proceed?
do i trust myself to make sound decisions?
do i let my heart lead?

do i even have space for this?
there's so much on my mind,
can i really be everything for her?
i guess i'll know in time.

polarity

green tea for you, cold brew for me.
i'll wear pink, you'd prefer black.
you're the masculine to my femininity,
you have the firmness that i lack.

i'm a bit more emotional, i've spiritually awoken.
you find it cute when i'm engulfed in a feeling.
you internalize a lot, i'm more outspoken,
but you're understanding with my healing.

there's a constant exchange of energy,
i give you mine, you give me yours.
you lift me out of my anxiety,
an endless love that pours.

we are so similar at baseline,
vibing at the same frequency,
we match emotions at the same time,
but handle them quite differently.

we bring awareness to new heights,
we share varying views.
curious of one another's insights,
receptive because there's nothing to prove.

there are many contrasts and it shows.
but communication is key.
we're here for all the highs and lows.
we've grown from this polarity.

you among the flowers

it's you among the flowers
standing on your own,
chasing the sun in every direction
perched upon your throne.

you radiate light,
the sun would ask to borrow.
it's dimming and overworked,
only you could raise it tomorrow.

you give everything you have
to those in desperate need of love,
it's a blessing for anyone to meet -
this flower that i write of.

the one with the honey eyes
the bees mistake for theirs,
their queen adjusts her crown,
this is a garden of your affairs.

you weren't always nurtured
or encouraged to blossom.
people came and went,
you made friends and you lost them.

yet you continued to flourish
settling roots in the dirt,
you've stood your ground in all weather,
and even moved on when it hurt.

no person can pluck you of your strength,
there is nothing that can hold you back.
that might be too much for some,
but that only speaks to what they lack.

so let me be here to support your growth,
i want to brighten all your hues,
because it's you among the flowers
that i will always choose.

stone

once a stranger now carrying my emotional
weight,
feeling my anguish and tasting the salt of my
tears,
doing all that you could so i wouldn't break,
validating my emotions and calming my fears.

i've held onto so much pain and self-doubt
and never valued myself.
i've literally struggled to leave the house
and thought i needed to be there for everyone
else.

you've encouraged me to do what makes me
happy,
regardless of how other people feel,
to make time for my passion of writing
and give myself space and time to heal.

i was experiencing so many emotions that
weren't mine.
i couldn't turn them off or escape.
i was also concerned i'd lose you over time,
i found myself drowning when it was too late.

fatigue, headache, i wasn't eating,
not taking care of my basic needs,
no sleep, having a hard time breathing,
withering and losing the light in me.

but you remained here listening, reaching for my hand,
to take on the things that i couldn't.
i lashed out, cried, and ran
out of fear you'd leave although you said you wouldn't.

this was happenstance, you came out of nowhere,
but also at the right time.
you showed me genuine love and care,
a beautiful gift from the divine.

i'm so grateful that you are the one,
reminding me that i'm never alone.
so thank you for all that you've done.
thank you for being my stone.

healing

all that has happened is definitely
worth the feeling,
of being awaken inside,
you've accelerated my healing.

the veil was broken
and you pulled me out of the dark.
i saw what i needed to do,
it only took that spark.

and now i know i'm capable,
because you helped me see,
that i can choose myself,
and love me unconditionally.

i can forgive what has happened
although it has hurt me deeply,
it doesn't cripple me anymore,
they can no longer reach me.

without your tender words,
endless love and support,
i wouldn't have evolved to
a better version i put forth.

so i dedicate this collection to you,
this journey, the ups and downs,
my heart will forever hold a space
for this special love that i have found.

sunflower #2

she thinks she's nothing special,
but tell her she's your world.
you love the way her dimple falls into her
cheeks,
and her head full of curls.

tell her she affects your heartbeat, your blood
pressure, she's part of your chemistry.
when she closes her eyes and her lashes meet,
it's you, you hope she's thinking of as she sleeps.

remind her of all the ways she's beautiful.
every freckle, her smile.
her skin so glowy and supple,
she'll catch you staring for a while.

and don't forget the way the light hits her eyes.
brown to amber, they're fire gold.
note all the purity she holds inside.
and keep the secrets that she has told.

tell her every day that you love her,
she's hardworking, strong, that you're proud.
don't assume she knows these things,
you need to say them out loud.

never let her feel alone.
don't let her crumble under stress.
be present, feed her soul,
ask her how to support her best.

be all that you have to,
to give her what she needs.
encourage her growth,
help her plant all those seeds.

praise her in all that she does
and watch her bloom.
she's your sunflower after all,
she's the light to your gloom.

alignment

elevens and ones are following me,
the twos are as well,
the weather allows me to take off,
555, i get my car and head to the hotel.

it's a full moon,
i pull out my cards for a reading.
truth, joy and passion,
two of cups prior knew where this was leading.

the elevator doors open,
and there you stand,
my spirit leaps forward,
my body follows on command.

pure love as i hold you for the first time,
closing my eyes and everyone fades away.
absorbing your warmth and feeling safe,
embracing eternity that day.

big kids running loose in a museum,
how perfectly your hand fits in mine,
avoiding the man in pink sherpa,
walking along you, side by side.

the art in the streets call me,
the architecture is amazing,
your beauty against the landscape,
i can’t help my gazing.

to hear you read classic poetry aloud
in a dusty corner bookstore,
dancing to queen in the aisle,
i didn’t know that i could love you more.

to feel your lips on mine,
that’s where they belong.
leaving myself on your skin,
the mark of a love song.

caressing your body on my way down,
licking your pores with my tongue,
your soft moans keep me going,
cleaning my mess when you’re done.

the sadness is real because our love is,
you tear first and i cry too.
the pain of separation is the worst,
not knowing the next time i’ll see you.

it took ten months for our paths to clear,
and the day finally arrived.
i wouldn’t change a thing about our journey,
or it wouldn’t have aligned.

nobody is going to love you the way i do,
you won't find a fraction of it anywhere else.
the lens i see you through is my own,
and maybe you just have to find out for yourself.

but we'll always have these hours,
chasing sunlight in philly,
i'll often think of the time,
when it was just you and me.

what i would do to be close again,
my heart aches to be your infinity.
there's not much i can do but wait,
and live in a weekend memory.

www.ingramcontent.com/pod-product-compliance
Lightning Source LLC
Chambersburg PA
CBHW051741130826
49812CB00033B/957
9789357440639